Manual of the
Eastern Star

Also from Westphalia Press

westphaliapress.org

Manual of the Eastern Star

Containing the Symbols, Scriptural Illustrations, Lectures, etc. Adapted to the System of Adoptive Masonry

by Robert Macoy

WESTPHALIA PRESS
An imprint of Policy Studies Organization

Westphalia Press
An imprint of Policy Studies Organization
1527 New Hampshire Ave., NW
Washington, D.C. 20036
info@ipsonet.org

ISBN-13: 978-1-63391-149-9
ISBN-10: 1633911497

Cover design by Taillefer Long at Illuminated Stories:
www.illuminatedstories.com

Daniel Gutierrez-Sandoval, Executive Director
PSO and Westphalia Press

Updated material and comments on this edition
can be found at the Westphalia Press website:
www.westphaliapress.org

MANUAL

OF THE ORDER OF THE

EASTERN STAR:

CONTAINING THE

SYMBOLS, SCRIPTURAL ILLUSTRATIONS, LECTURES, ETC.,

ADAPTED TO THE SYSTEM OF

ADOPTIVE MASONRY.

ARRANGED BY

ROBERT MACOY,

NATIONAL GRAND SECRETARY.

———————— ◆◆◆ ————————

"I HAVE SEEN HIS STAR IN THE EAST,
AND HAVE COME TO WORSHIP HIM."

———————— ◆◆◆ ————————

𝔅𝔢𝔞𝔲𝔱𝔦𝔣𝔲𝔩𝔩𝔶 𝔍𝔩𝔩𝔲𝔰𝔱𝔯𝔞𝔱𝔢𝔡.

NEW YORK:

MASONIC PUBLISHING AND MANUFACTURING COMPANY,

432 BROOME STREET.

CHICAGO:—J. C. W. BAILEY.

1866.

ADOPTIVE RITE;

OR,

FEMALE FREEMASONRY.

———◆———

HISTORICAL SKETCH.

ECRET societies, imitating Freemasonry, for the admission of females as members were first organized in France during the early part of the eighteenth century, and still exist there and in other parts of Europe as a distinctive Rite.

By the term *Adoptive Masonry* is implied that system of forms, ceremonies, and explanatory lectures which is communicated to certain classes of ladies, who, from their relationship by blood or marriage to Master Masons in good standing, are entitled to the respect and attention of the entire Fraternity.

These ladies are said to be *adopted* into the Masonic communion, because the system of forms, ceremonies, and lectures above referred to enables them to express their wishes, and gives satisfactory evidence of their claims, in a manner that no stranger to the Masonic family can do.

To the organizations thus established for the initiation of females the French have given the name of "Adoptive Masonry," *Maçonnerie d' Adoption,* and the Lodges are called *Loges d' Adoption,* or "Adoptive Lodges," because every Lodge of females was obliged to be adopted by, and under the guardianship of, some regular Masonic Lodge.

One of the first of these societies was the "Order of Perfect Happiness," for so we may be permitted to translate the name of "Felicitaires," which they adopted. This society assumed a nautical character in its emblems and its vocabulary. It was divided into the four degrees of "Cabin-Boy," "Master," "Commodore," and "Vice-Admiral." What little information we have been enabled to obtain from a very brief notice of its ritual leads us to believe that it was not of a character to merit countenance. It did not long retain its existence; for two years after its formation it gave place to the "Knights and Heroines of the Anchor," which was, however, but a refinement of the original society, and preserved its formula of initiation, and nearly all its ceremonies.

In 1747, one Beauchaine, the Master of one of the Parisian Lodges, instituted a new society, which he called "L'Ordre des Fendeurs," or the Order of Wood-cutters. This institution borrowed its principal ceremonies from the society of the Carbonari, or Coal-burners, which had been previously established in Italy. The place of meeting of the Wood-cutters was called the "wood-yard," and was supposed to represent a forest; the presiding officer was called "Father Master," and the male and female members were styled "Cousins." This society became at once exceedingly popular, and the most distinguished ladies and gentlemen of France united themselves to it. It was, consequently, the cause of the institution of many similar societies, such as the Order of the Hatchet, of Fidelity, etc.

In consequence of the increasing popularity of the numerous secret associations, which, in their external characters and mysterious rites, attempted an imitation of Freemasonry, differing, however, from that institution, of which they were, perhaps, the rivals for public favor, by the admission of female members, the Grand Orient of France, in 1774, established a new rite, called the "Rite of Adoption," which was placed under the control of the Grand Orient. Rules and regulations were thenceforth provided for the government of these Lodges of Adoption, one of which was that no men should be permitted to attend them except regular Freemasons, and that each Lodge should be placed under the charge, and held under the sanction and warrant, of some regularly constituted Masonic Lodge, whose Master, or, in his absence, his Deputy, should be the presiding officer, assisted by a female President or Mistress. Under these regulations a Lodge of Adoption was opened in Paris, in 1775, under the patronage of the Lodge of St. Anthony, and in which the Duchess of Bourbon presided, and was installed as Grand Mistress of the Adoptive rite.

Many systems of Adoptive Masonry have, from time to time, been introduced in the United States, with varied success, none of which, however, seemed to possess the elements of permanency, except the Order of the EASTERN STAR, which was established in this country during the year 1778. The success of this Order, therefore, corresponds in its beneficence and usefulness with the extent of Freemasonry. Its obligations are based upon the honor of the female sex; and framed upon the principles of EQUALITY and JUSTICE; that whatever benefits are due by the Masonic Fraternity *to* the wives, widows, daughters and sisters of Masons, corresponding benefits are due *from* them to the members of the Masonic Fraternity.

The theory of the Order of the EASTERN STAR is founded upon the Holy Writings. Five prominent female characters, illustrating as many Masonic virtues, are selected, *adopted* and placed under Masonic protection. The selections are:

1. JEPHTHAH'S DAUGHTER, illustrating *respect to the binding force of a vow ;*

2. RUTH, illustrating *devotion to religious principles ;*

3. ESTHER, illustrating *fidelity to kindred and friends ;*

4. MARTHA, illustrating *undeviating faith in the hour of trial ;*

5. ELECTA, illustrating *patience and submission under wrongs.*

These are all Masonic virtues, and have nowhere in history more brilliant exemplars than in the five characters illustrated in the lectures of the Order of the EASTERN STAR.

The honorable and exalted purposes, had in view in its dissemination, can have no opposition worthy the name. Its effects in winning to the advocacy of Masonry the virtuous, intelligent and influential lady members of our families are truly encouraging, and stimulate its friends to persevere in a general promulgation of the system.

According to the tenets of the Order of the EASTERN STAR, Adoptive Masonry stands a bright monument to female secrecy and fidelity, and proves how wrong all those are who fancy a woman is not to be trusted. There is not in the whole of the ceremonies of this Rite a single point with which the most ascetic moralist could find fault. On the contrary, all is pure, all is beautiful; it is among the brightest jewels which spangle the records of Masonry.

As the adoptive privileges of the lady entirely depend upon the good standing and affiliation of the Brother through whom she is introduced, this system will be a strong inducement, it is thought, to keep a Brother, otherwise inclined to err, within the bounds of morality.

A general diffusion of this Rite will tend to supersede the other so-called *Female Degrees*, as being, at the best, but trivial, and, henceforth, superfluous and useless.

RULES

FOR THE GOVERNMENT OF THE ORDER OF THE

EASTERN STAR.

I. Not less than five ladies who are entitled to receive, or have received, the degrees should be present at any communication when the degrees of this Order are conferred.

II. The proper persons entitled to receive the degrees are :

1. All MASTER MASONS in good standing ;
2. The WIVES of Master Masons in good standing ;
3. The WIDOWS of Master Masons who died in good standing ;
4. The SISTERS of Master Masons in good standing ;
5. The DAUGHTERS of Master Masons in good standing.

III. Those who are not entitled to receive the degrees are :

1. Unmarried ladies, if under 18 years of age ;
2. Mothers of Masons.
3. Half-sisters or Step-daughters ;
4. Master Masons who may stand expelled, suspended, or against whom charges may be pending.

IV. Each person before acquiring a knowledge of the degrees must be honorably pledged to the observance of the above rules, and to the strictest discretion in regard to the essential secrets of the degrees.

V. A well-guarded apartment must be secured for conferring the degrees.

———

No person should aspire to the office of INSTRUCTOR until he has thoroughly qualified himself for the work by imprinting the Lectures upon his memory; perfecting himself in the Signs, Passwords and Scriptural Illustrations; and securing confidence in himself, so that he may not become confused when he rises to address an audience.

The INSTRUCTOR should make the Lecture graceful, dignified and impressive. No one should be allowed to enter the room after the pledge of secrecy has been imparted.

These requisitions being complied with, the Brother who may be acting as INSTRUCTOR will proceed upon the general plan indicated in this volume; that is, he will make allusions, by way of opening, to the history, extent and purposes of Freemasonry; its claims to the respect and attachment of the ladies; and the practical objects for which the Order of the EASTERN STAR was instituted.

OPENING ODE.

In which the audience are requested to join.

Words by Rob. Morris, LL.D.
Arranged by Bro. Henry Tucker.

Music published by permission
of Root & Cady, Chicago.

Air :—*Just Before the Battle, Mother.*

Here a - round the al - tar meet - ing,

Where the sons of light com - bine;

Min - gled with our friend - ly greet - ing,

Is the glow of love di - vine;

For this Hall to vir - tue giv - en,
Cho. Keep in view the Lodge su - pern - al,

And our em - blems on the wall,
Life is love en - thron'd in Heav'n,

Point us to the Lodge in Heav - en
Where the true light nev - er wav - ers

And the Mas - ter of us all.
And our mor - tal sins for - given.

In the bonds of Mason's *duty*,
  Seek we now the Mason's *light*,
Forms of Wisdom, Strength and Beauty
· ·Teach us what is good and right ;
Far be every sinful passion,
  Near be every gentle grace ;
And so at last this holy mission
  Shall reveal our MASTER's face.

CHORUS.—Keep in view the Lodge supernal,
      Life is love enthroned in Heaven,
    Where the true light never wavers,
    And our mortal sins forgiven.

  After the Ode is sung the INSTRUCTOR will recite
the following

WELCOME.

A welcome and a greeting now,
   To gentle friends and sisters true,
Around the place where Masons bow,
      And pay their homage due ;
On CHECKERED FLOOR, 'neath STARRY SKY,
Welcome, kind friends of Masonry!

To her who finds a FATHER here ;
   Or BROTHER's strong and trusty hand ;
To her who mourns the lost and dear,
      Once cherished in our band ;
To her who HUSBAND's love doth own,
Greeting and Welcome, every one!

Welcome the *light* our emblems shed ;
   Welcome the *hopes* yon volume gives—
Welcome the *love* our Covenants spread,
      The *wages* each receives ;
And when is past life's toilsome week,
Welcome the HOME that Masons seek.

The Welcome having been recited, the IN-STRUCTOR will open the lectures of the EASTERN STAR in the following or similar language:

ADDRESS.

ADIES:—We meet and welcome you here for a double purpose. *First,* that we may inform you as to your true relationship to the Masonic Fraternity, and thus remove any prejudices that you may have entertained against us; and *Second,* to confer upon you the beautiful, instructive and useful Degrees of the Order of the EASTERN STAR.

Every one present knows that Freemasons set a great value upon their mysteries. They put themselves to much trouble and expense to attend their Lodges, and they prove by their words and actions that Masonry is implanted in their affections. It must be plain enough to every wife and daughter, and sister of a Mason, that there is something in Masonry, known only to the brethren, which is very delightful and precious to them. This oftentimes provokes the question, *of what use is Masonry to the Ladies?* As it separates man and wife to some extent, by giving the man certain secrets and duties which the wife cannot share, the ladies sometimes take umbrage against Masonry, and even become its enemies, and oppose it violently as something contrary to the laws of God and man. A little knowledge, however, *of the real nature and purposes of Masonry* will remove all this, if there is any of it existing in the mind of any lady present.

Masons love and cherish their society above all others, because it is designed to, and does, make them better, wiser and happier men. *Better*, for it teaches morality, virtue, temperance, economy, charity and justice to all men. *Wiser*, for it imparts knowledge to them that is weighty, solemn and important; knowledge that has been handed down to them from age to age for nearly three thousand years. *Happier*, for it makes them acquainted with and puts them in social connection with the purest and best men in every section of the country. Is it any wonder, then, ladies, that Masons love Masonry?

If a Mason is assailed in character, every other Mason is or should be prompt to defend him, if innocent. If he is attacked in person, he finds defenders. If he is distressed for means, poor and in want, having been reduced by misfortune, his brethren share their abundance with him. If traveling in a foreign land he falls sick, or in distress, though all around him may be strangers, *the Masons are no strangers to him. They are Brothers*, and will be as kind to him as though they had known him all his life. If he dies, the Fraternity will bear his body to its last resting place and drop an honest tear to his memory.

But now it is necessary that we should show you· why ladies too should love Masonry, and should be, as many‿of them are, *its warmest friends and defenders.* I will answer the question that is often asked, *of what use is Masonry to the female sex?*

Ladies, you are connected with Masonry by ties far more intimate and tender than you are aware of, or than I can even inform you of. The widow and orphan daughter of a Master Mason takes the place of the husband and father in the affections and good deeds of the Lodge. If their character is unjustly assailed, the brethren are in duty bound to defend them. If they are in want, distressed for the necessities of life, the brethren will divide their means with them. If traveling at a distance from home they find themselves sick and in want, among strangers, they have but to make themselves known as the widow and the orphan daughter of a worthy Master Mason, and lo, the hand of relief is stretched out toward them! The kind voice of sympathy is heard to cheer them! They are no longer strangers, but friends, dear friends, and thus they are constrained to bless our society, whose kind deeds are not confined to the narrow limits of home.

Ladies, I draw no fancy sketch, I speak of what has happened, of what is happening every day. The Widow has been provided with a home, her children educated and reared up to honorable stations, her own heart cheered and comforted by the blessed influences of Masonry.

These, then, ladies, are the reasons why we think you should be the most devoted friends that Masonry possesses. To you are given all the advantages of the society, its shield of protection, its hand of relief, and its voice of sympathy, while we do not require of you any of the labor or expense of sustaining it. The only Masonic privilege denied to you is that of *visiting the Lodge*, and this would be of no advantage to you, even if it were possible to grant it, but it would awaken the voice of scandal against you from a censorious world, and thus produce far more pain to your kind and amiable hearts than it could possibly afford you pleasure. *Females cannot be made Masons.* This is a rule that has been handed down with the other rules of Masonry for thousands of years. Each Mason present pledged himself before he was admitted into the Lodge that he would never allow any of the ancient rules of Masonry to be changed, and this is one of them. Therefore we cannot invite you to visit our Lodges. But, as I have. said, we can, and do, and will share with you in all the solid privileges and benefits of Masonry, and thus practically unite you with us in this great, this glorious, this heavenly work of doing good.

The only objection that can be advanced against what I have said is this: how is a lady, traveling among strangers, and finding herself in want of friends, to make herself known as the wife, widow, sister or daughter of a Master Mason? Unless she has something more than her mere word to offer those to whom she applies will be slow to believe her statements. The country is full of impostors, women as well as men. Almost every charitable person has been imposed upon, not once only, but many times. The lady, therefore, who has the relationship to Masonry that you possess needs, in such a case, some particular means of recognition; some means of *making herself known to Master Masons*, which no other person can understand; some method, perfect, modest, and proper, easily practiced and easily understood. Is there anything of this sort? I imagine you asking me. Are there any means, long tried and proved, which a lady can learn, and by due practice remember, so that, if suddenly called upon, she can put it into use with confidence that it will prove effectual? I answer there *is just such a method*, and one principal object of this meeting is to teach you that method. The Order is called the EASTERN STAR. It has signs and pass-words, and means of recognition which have been tried in a thousand instances, and proved to be exactly what a lady needs in the cases I have mentioned. The signs which are for a lady's use are easily learned and remembered. The pass-words which Masons use in answer to the signs are equally so. The other means of recognition, by the aid of the Signet, are not easily forgotten, and the whole system is available for practical use at all times when required.

And there is one great merit in the Order of the EASTERN STAR, which, if there were no other, would render it worthy of your favor; *it is pure, graceful, and religious.* It gives the history of that heroic daughter of JEPHTHAH, doomed to die for her father's sake. It tells us of RUTH, the harvest gleaner in the field of Boaz, who forsook all things to dwell among the people of God. It speaks of ESTHER, that noble daughter of bondage, who so bravely resolved to share the fortunes of the exiles of Israel. It tells us of MARTHA, mourning the loss of her dearly beloved brother. And, finally, it thrills us with an account of that devoted philanthropist, ELECTA, who above all women suffered for her Master's sake, the loss of home, family, wealth, and life itself.

But before I can communicate to you the secrets of the EASTERN STAR Degrees whereby you can make yourselves known to Masons, it is necessary that each of you should make a solemn pledge of honor, that those secrets shall be kept inviolably in your possession. For any one of you to go out and expose to others what we so secretly tell you here would not only be FATAL to your own character for truth, but would destroy all the advantages of the Order itself. Its great value consists in its being kept in the hands of proper persons. I am happy to inform you that although many thousands of ladies have received it, and they, scattered through every section of the country, no instance is on record of any lady having dishonorably exposed it. Nor, indeed, do we fear that such a misfortune can ever occur. A lady who makes us a pledge of honor, such as I require of you, pledges her very soul; the honor of a woman is more to her than life itself. Those of you, therefore, who give us such security may safely be trusted with our most cherished secrets.

The pledge that we require of you is in this form:

So many of you, ladies, as will pledge the sacred honor of a woman never to communicate improperly the secrets of the Order of the EASTERN STAR, *will raise your right hands.* [See that each one does it.]

My Brethren! I have thus far confined my remarks to the ladies, whose coming together on this occasion we may justly feel to be a compliment to us. *You* know and can testify that all my statements as to the principles of Masonry and its advantages to its members are true, and that these ladies *do* stand in the close relationship to our Fraternity that I have described. I will now explain to you that none but the Wives, Widows, Sisters, and Daughters of Master Masons—the Sisters and Daughters if unmarried to be eighteen years of age and upward—are entitled to receive the EASTERN STAR Degrees, and that it must never be conferred unless there are five or more such ladies present:

So many of you, my Brethren, as will pledge the honor of a Master Mason never to confer or be present at the conferring of the EASTERN STAR Degrees, except under the restrictions mentioned, will raise your right hands. [See that each one does it.]

Should a lady, at any time, find herself in distress, and among strangers, she has the undeniable right, and should not hesitate, to make the acquaintance of any Master Mason who may be present, by using one of the signs which I will teach you. Each sign has its appropriate name and explanation, and each has a proper password to be given in answer to it by the Mason who recognizes the sign.

The first object to which I call your attention is *the Signet of the* EASTERN STAR. This is prepared with a view to assist the memory after a person

has taken the Degrees.   You will observe that the
Star in the Signet is *five-pointed,* and that each
point has a color of its own, which are blue,
yellow, white, green, and red.   The names of
the five characters, JEPHTHAH'S DAUGHTER, RUTH,
ESTHER, MARTHA, and ELECTA, are seen in the dif-
ferent points, and their histories make up the
Degrees. The emblems—the Sword and the Vail,
the Sheaf, the Crown and the Scepter, the Broken
Column, and the Joined Hands—on the same
points, are illustrative of the above characters.

The emblems in the several divisions in the
center of the Star also allude to the distinguished
characters composing the Degrees. 1st. The
Open Bible is appropriate to JEPHTHAH'S DAUGH-
TER, as the symbol of obedience to the Word of
God.   2d. The Bunch of Lilies is appropriate
to RUTH, as the Lily of the Valley.   3d. The Sun
is appropriate to ESTHER, as the effulgent sun is
the symbol of crowned majesty.   4th. The Lamb
is appropriate to MARTHA, as the symbol of innocence, faith, and humility.   5th. The Lion is
appropriate to ELECTA, as the symbol of the
courage and power which sustained her during
her severe trials.

THE FIRST POINT.

JEPHTHAH'S DAUGHTER;

OR, THE DAUGHTER'S DEGREE.

The Symbol of the Vail.

She will not die as thief or murderer dies
　Whose fate but expiates his horrid crime ;
She will not vail her pure and loving eyes
　As fearing death, for hers is death sublime ;
Lo, with determined heart and eye she stands,
Her face upturned toward Celestial lands !

Scriptural Illustration.

And it came to pass, when he saw her, that he rent his clothes, and said, Alas, my daughter! thou hast brought me very low, and thou art one of them that trouble me ; for I have opened my mouth unto the Lord, and I cannot go back.—JUDGES xi., 35.

COLOR—**Blue.**—Represented by the *Violet*. Its retired, shrinking nature is emblematical of JEPHTHAH'S DAUGHTER, the devoted maid of Mizpeh.

EMBLEMS:—The Sword and the Vail.

I HAVE SEEN HIS STAR IN THE EAST,
AND HAVE COME TO WORSHIP HIM.

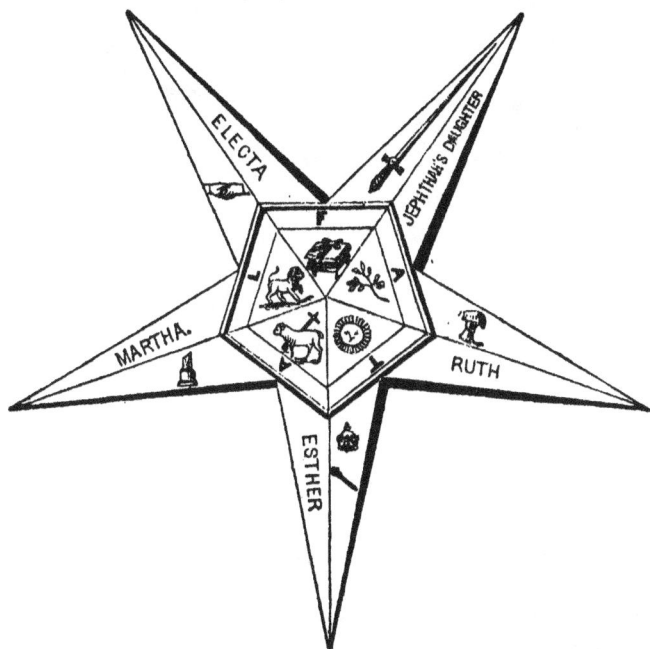

𝕱. 𝕬. 𝕿. 𝕬. 𝕷.

FAIREST of Souls above
    Are those who suffered here ;
They gave the sacrifice of Love
    To prove their hearts sincere.

JEPHTHAH'S DAUGHTER.

FIRST DEGREE.

THE structure of Freemasonry, in its obligations and principles is peculiar, and we, as Master Masons, are taught *to respect the binding force of a vow.* Therefore, when we find in Bible history a person who submits to wrongs, to suffering and death, *to secure the sanctity of a vow,* we seize upon that character as our own.

We adopt or surround it with fraternal protection. We hail it as a Masonic character, and we claim whatever credit or honor may be associated with it.

Such a character, forcibly delineated, we discover in the Book of Judges, under the title of JEPHTHAH'S DAUGHTER. And we have so surrounded the SACRIFICE of that noble and heroic woman with emblems, legends and tokens of recognition as to make of it a section in ADOPTIVE MASONRY.

The history of JEPHTHAH'S DAUGHTER, as composing a Degree of the EASTERN STAR, is thus given:

Her father, JEPHTHAH, was a resident of Mizpeh, in the mountains of Gilead, a warrior, and a man of decided personal character.

Being called upon, in the extremity of his country's trials, to go at the head of its armies and resist the Ammonites, its enemies, he prepared his household for a campaign that would perhaps cost him his life, and then committed himself to the protection of God in solemn prayer. It was an age when religious knowledge was scanty and man knew but little of his Maker's will. JEPHTHAH thought to propitiate Deity by a vow, such as his forefathers had made when about to depart upon dangerous enterprises. And this is the record of his vow as found in the XIth Chapter of the Book of Judges:

Jephthah uttered all his words before the Lord in Mizpeh.

And Jephthah vowed a vow unto the Lord, and said, If thou shalt without fail deliver the children of Ammon into mine hands,

Then it shall be that whatsoever cometh forth of the doors of my house to meet me, when I return in peace from the children of Ammon, shall surely be the Lord's, and I will OFFER IT UP FOR A BURNT-OFFERING.

It is difficult to explain this vow. It has been conjectured that being a hunter in the mountains of Gilead JEPHTHAH was accustomed to be much absent from home, and that on his return from those expeditions he was often welcomed by the favorite lamb of his daughter; and that this fact was in his mind suggesting the object of sacrifice, should his present dangerous enterprise be crowned with success. This explanation is accepted as the best at our command. JEPHTHAH went forth to battle, expecting if victorious to make a thank-offering to GOD of the pet lamb of his daughter.

The victory was gained, and the warrior returned to Mizpeh exulting in his success. God had redeemed his people. The thanks and praises of a grateful nation were showered upon his track. The loving father hastened home to enjoy the congratulations of his neighbors and still more of his daughter—his only child.

Arrived upon the hill which overlooked his dwelling, he halted. For now the full purport of his vow broke in upon his mind. The Lord had "without fail delivered the children of Ammon into his hands;" he had returned in peace to his house," and whatever "came forth of the doors of his nouse, to meet him, must be the Lord's to be offered up for a burnt-offering."

It was but for a moment. The door opened as his eye painfully regarded it. It opened and something came forth; not a pet lamb, not even a servant or a neighbor; but his daughter, his only child, the object in whom his very existence was bound up. "Behold," says the sacred narrative, "his daughter came out to meet him with timbrels and with dances." Jephthah rent his clothes and in the anguish of his heart cried aloud, "Alas, my daughter! thou hast brought me very low. I have opened my mouth to the Lord, and I cannot go back."

ADAH was a daughter in every way worthy of that warrior-sire, the mighty hunter of Gilead. Casting away the instruments of rejoicing, and changing the merry dance to solemn measures, she answered: "My father, if thou hast opened thy mouth unto the LORD, do to me according to that which hath proceeded out of thy mouth." She had but one request to make, and she was ready for the sacrifice. She asked that she might go among the mountains for two months, and there, with the virgins of Israel, prepare her mind to meet in calmness and resignation her impending doom. The request was granted, and during two revolving moons the heroic woman joined in the hymns and prayers of her friends, with which the mountain caves of Gilead became vocal.

When the two months had expired, and the day arrived which was to bring this sad affair to a close, a vast multitude gathered together to witness the event. Precisely as the sun came on the meridian she was seen, followed by a long train of her friends, winding their way down the mountain's side, to the fatal spot where the altar was erected, and her father with an almost broken heart was standing, prepared to fulfill his vow.

She approached him and with one long kiss of affection bade him farewell. Taking up the thick mourning vail which she had worn, he threw it gently over her face and drew his sword. But she rapidly unvailed herself, and said she needed not to have her face covered, for *she was not afraid to die.* Her father replied that he could not strike the blow while she looked upon him, and again cast it over her. She threw it off the second time, and turning from him said she would look up to the heavens, so that his hand should not be unnerved by the sight of her face, but that *she would not consent to die in the dark.* A third time, however, he insisted, and a third time she as resolutely cast it off, this time HOLDING THE ENDS OF IT FIRMLY IN HER HANDS, and. then in the hearing of the multitude she solemnly declared that if this ceremony was insisted upon she would claim the protection of the law and refuse the fate that otherwise she was willing to endure. She said it was the practice to cover the faces of murderers and criminals when they were about to be put to death, but for her part *she was no criminal, and died only to redeem her father's honor.* Again she averred that she would cast her eyes upward upon the source of Light, and in that position she invited the fatal blow. It fell. Her gentle spirit mounted to the heavens upon which her last gaze had been fixed, and so the deed was consummated which has rendered the name of JEPHTHAH'S DAUGHTER forever famous in the annals of Scripture.

For hundreds of years, and even down to the time of SAMUEL, "it was a custom in Israel that the daughters of Israel went yearly to lament the daughter of JEPHTHAH, the Gileadite, four days in the year."

The color BLUE alludes to the cerulean hue of the mountains in whose solitude JEPHTHAH'S DAUGHTER passed two months while preparing herself for death.

The EMBLEM of the SWORD reminds us of the instrument of her death.

The SIGN alludes   *   *   *

The PASS is used to recall the lamentable but glorious event to which the entire history of JEPHTHAH'S DAUGHTER refers.

TRIBUTE TO JEPHTHAH'S DAUGHTER.

See 'midst the multitude the VICTIM stands!
　Dauntless, serene, though terror palsies them!
And she must die by her own father's hands!
　And she must die a sacrifice of shame!
Of shame? ah, no! she flings the vail abroad,
Once, twice, yea thrice; looks hopefully to God;
Fixes the noonday sun with earnest eyes,
Then crowned with innocence, the Maiden dies!

Lament for JEPHTHAH, ye who know his fate,
　Weep and lament; "Broken the beautiful rod,
And the strong staff; Mizpeh is desolate!"
　But for sweet ADAH weep not; let the word
Be: "Joy to the Captive, freed from earthly dust,
Joy for one witness more to woman's trust,
And lasting honor, Mizpeh, be the strain
　To HER WHO DIED IN LIGHT without a stain!"

THE SECOND POINT.

RUTH;

OR, THE WIDOW'S DEGREE

The Symbol of the Ripened Grain.

Pity the widow, desolate and poor ;
Those little parcels are her only store ;
Meekly upon her breast she crosses them,
Prophetic of the Cross of Bethlehem ;
Then looks, imploringly, into the sky,
Where sits enthroned the pitying Deity.

Scriptural Illustration.

Then said BOAZ unto his servant that was set over the reapers, Whose damsel is this?—RUTH ii., 5.

COLOR—*Yellow.*—Represented by the *Sunflower*, emblematical of the ripened grain gleaned by RUTH, the pious widow of Moab.

EMBLEM :—The Sheaf.

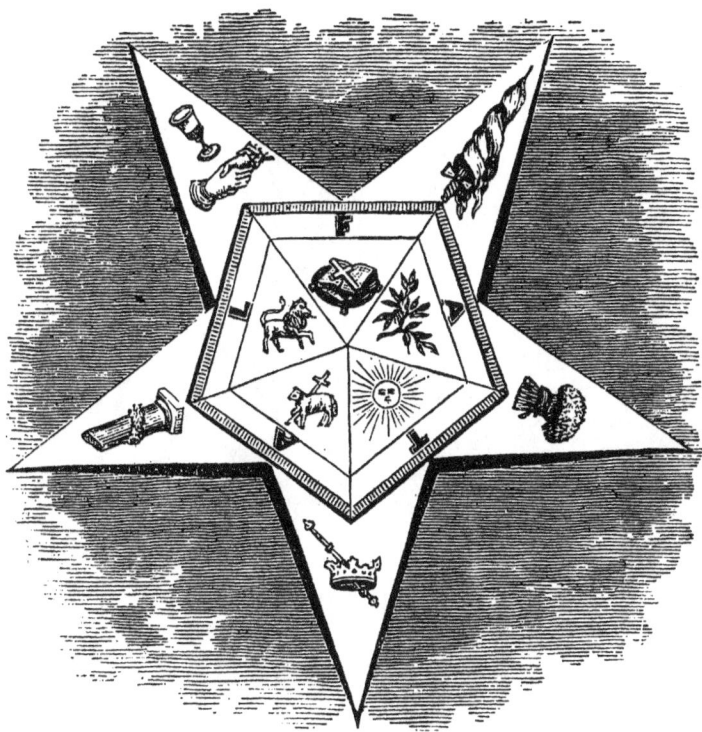

I have seen his Star in the East,
And have come to Worship Him.

F. A. T. A. L.

AMONG the ranks of earth
Our noblest oft are hid ;
But God will call his chosen forth,
And crown the humble head.

RUTH.

REEMASONRY, in its obligations, emblems and principles, is peculiar, and we, as Master Masons, are taught to *respect devotion to religious principles.* Upon our first entrance into the Masonic Lodge we testify our faith and trust in GOD. Atheism will effectually debar any person from becoming a Freemason.

Therefore, when we find in history a person who forsakes home, and lands, and parents, and country, *through piety to God*, we seize upon that character, and hail it as Masonic; and we claim whatever credit or honor may be associated with it.

Such a character, forcibly delineated, we discover in the Book of Ruth, under the title of RUTH. And we have so surrounded the PIETY of that noble and heroic woman with emblems, legends, and tokens of recognition, as to make of it a section in ADOPTIVE MASONRY.

The history of RUTH, as composing a Degree of the EASTERN STAR, is as follows:

RUTH was of the nation of Moab, an idolatrous people. She married a man named MAHLON, formerly a citizen of Bethlehem, who had taken up his residence in the land of Moab, where he died. He was a worshiper of GOD, and by his pious example and teachings she was converted to the true religion. A few happy years followed, and then the calamity of widowhood came upon her. Upon his death-bed he solemnly exhorted her, for her soul's sake, to leave the dangerous company in which she would be thrown, and go to the city of Bethlehem, where dwelt the people of GOD.

Immediately after his death she obeyed his pious injunctions. Forsaking her home and friends, she journeyed in company with her aged mother-in-law to Bethlehem, where she arrived in due time, way-worn and so poor that she was compelled, for her own support and that of her friend, to seek some means of securing a livelihood. There was nothing, however, that she could do, save to go into the barley fields—for it was the time of harvest—and glean among the poorest and lowest classes of the people for a support. The very first attempt she made at this labor exhausted her strength. She had been reared in luxury, and the toil was too great for her. The sharp stubble wounded her feet. The blazing sun oppressed her brain. The jeers and insults of her companions alarmed and discouraged her, and long before the hour of noon, with only two little handsful of barley, as the fruits of her labor, she sought the shade of a tree to rest herself for a few moments before retiring from the field.

At this instant BOAZ, the owner of the field, entered. He was a pious and charitable man. None in Bethlehem was so rich, none more beloved and honored than he. As he entered the field, he observed near the gleaners the form of one differing in garb and manners from the rest, and asked the overseer who she was? In reply he learned that she was a woman from Moab, who had asked leave to glean among the sheaves, but that evidently she was unaccustomed to such labor, for she had been there since the sunrise, and had gathered but two little handsful of barley. This excited the kindly feelings of Boaz, and he went to her to say a word of sympathy, and to offer her relief.

As she saw him approach, she supposed him to be the owner of the field, and come to order her away. Ever since the morning she had met nothing but scorn and reproach, and she looked for it now. RAISING HER HANDS, therefore, to show him how small were her gleanings, and that she had taken nothing from the sheaves, she CROSSED THEM MEEKLY UPON HER BREAST, as showing her willingness to submit to whatever lot she might be called upon to endure, and CAST HER EYES UPWARD as appealing to GOD against the inhumanity of man. It was for GOD she had forsaken home, wealth and friends, and the disconsolate widow, alone in the world, had none other to whom she could look for protection. This mute appeal was not lost upon the kind heart of Boaz. He spoke words of sympathy and tenderness to her. He encouraged her to persevere. From the provisions brought for his reapers he bade her eat and drink. He directed that handsful of barley should be dropped on purpose in her way by the reapers, so that she might gather an ample supply; and when she returned home, to her mother-in-law, she bore with her enough for their immediate necessities. In a short time RUTH became the wife of BOAZ, by whom she had a son, called OBED, the father of JESSE, the father of DAVID, the father of SOLOMON, whose wisdom and power are known to every intelligent Freemason.

The color YELLOW alludes to the ripened grain that composed the barley sheaves of BOAZ, among which RUTH was gleaning.

The EMLLEM of the SHEAF reminds us of the liberality of BOAZ, who, from his sheaves, commanded that portions be taken and cast in RUTH's way, that she might gather an abundance.

The SIGN alludes *   *   *

The PASS is used to recall the then lowering but afterwards glorious history of the heroic RUTH.

TRIBUTE TO RUTH.

Widow, mourning for the dead,
'Midst the golden harvest mourning,
   Beats the sun thy aching head?
   Burns the stubble neath thy tread?
No kind look thy gaze returning?
   These poor parcels all thy store?
   Surely God will give thee more!

Stand, then, mournfully and sigh;
Raise thy hands in meek submission;
   Thy Redeemer, RUTH, is nigh—
   Marks thee with a gracious eye,
Knows thy lonely, sad condition:
   All thou'st given him and more
   Shall be rendered from his store!

THE THIRD POINT.

———o⟶∘⟨⟩∘⟨o———

ESTHER;

OR, THE WIFE'S DEGREE.

———∘⟨⟩∘———

𝕿𝖍𝖊 𝕾𝖞𝖒𝖇𝖔𝖑 𝖔𝖋 𝖙𝖍𝖊 𝕮𝖗𝖔𝖜𝖓 𝖆𝖓𝖉 𝖙𝖍𝖊 𝕾𝖈𝖊𝖕𝖙𝖊𝖗.

Nobly she stands, a Queen: the glittering band
Mark of a royal state beneath her hand:
She points the silken robe with peerless grace,
Pure as her soul and pallid as her face;
Then reaches to the Scepter whence is drawn
The kingly pardon she has bravely won.

———∘⟨⟩∘———

Scriptural Illustration.

Then said the King unto her, What wilt thou, Queen
ESTHER? and what is thy request? It shall be even given
thee to the half of the kingdom.—ESTHER v., 3.

———∘⟨⟩∘———

COLOR—**White.**—Represented by the *White Lily,*
emblematical of the white robes of ESTHER, the noble-
hearted Queen of Persia.

EMBLEMS:—The Crown and the Scepter.

𝕴 have seen his 𝕾tar in the 𝕰ast,
𝕬nd have come to 𝕸orship 𝕳im.

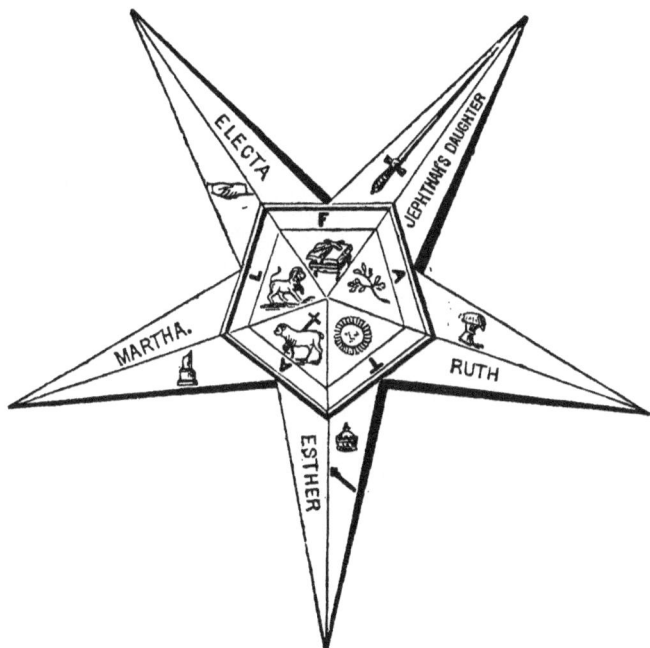

𝕱. 𝕬. 𝕿. 𝕬. 𝕷.

Tᴇɴ ᴛʜᴏᴜsᴀɴᴅ anxious thoughts
    Do oft our prayers oppress ;
But he who reigns in heavenly courts
    Will surely hear and bless.

ESTHER.

THIRD DEGREE.

THE principles and obligations of Freemasonry are fraternal, and we, as Master Masons, are taught to *respect fidelity to kindred and friends.* We are introduced into Freemasonry by a *friend,* vouched for by a *friend,* conducted by a *friend.* Friendly hands support us through life, close our eyes in death, and consign us tenderly to the bosom of mother earth. There is no offense in Masonry more degrading than a breach of friendship.

Therefore, when we find in history a person, exalted in station, rich in this world's goods, learned and beloved, who casts all these advantages aside in *her fidelity to kindred and friends,* we seize upon that character as our own. We adopt and protect it. We hail it as a Masonic character, and we claim whatever credit or honor may be associated with it.

Such a character, forcibly delineated, we discover in the Book of ESTHER, under the title of ESTHER. And we have so surrounded the EFFORTS of that noble and heroic woman with emblems, legends and tokens of recognition as to make of it a section in ADOPTIVE MASONRY.

The history of ESTHER, as composing a Degree of the EASTERN STAR, is thus given:

Her husband, AHASUERUS, otherwise termed ARTAXERXES, was King of Persia, a monarch of vast power, a man faithful to his word, and devotedly attached to the queen-consort.

The heroine, ESTHER, was a Jewish damsel of the tribe of BENJAMIN. The family had not returned to Judea after the permission given by CYRUS, and she was born beyond the Tigris, about five hundred years before the Christian era. Her parents being dead, MORDECAI, her uncle, took care of her education. After AHASUERUS had divorced Queen VASHTI, search was made throughout Persia for the most beautiful women, and ESTHER was one selected. She found favor in the eyes of the King, who married her with royal magnificence, bestowing largesses and remissions of tribute on his people.

Her matchless beauty having attracted the attention of the King; her virtues secured his love, but her wonderful genius gained his permanent admiration and respect. No woman has ever left behind her a better record of wisdom than ESTHER. It is a standing tradition among her people that *as Solomon was to men so was Esther to women*, the wisest of her sex. The more intimately the King became acquainted with her mental powers the more he respected them. There was no problem of state so intricate that she could not aid him to solve. In time she became his confidant, and shared with him in the greatness of the kingdom. These circumstances enabled her in a season of peril to save her nation from destruction.

The enemies of the Jews, who were numerous

and powerful, had brought false accusations before the King, and persuaded him to utter an edict that, upon a fixed day, the entire race throughout all Persia should be exterminated. The chosen people of GOD were doomed to be extirpated from the face of the country. The instrument to avert so great a calamity was the heroine, ESTHER.

No sooner did she learn of this cruel edict than she promptly resolved to save her people or perish in the same destruction. The King had often admitted his indebtedness to her counsels, and pledged his royal word to grant her any request she might make of him, even "to the half of the kingdom," and ESTHER now resolved to test his sincerity, and appeal to him, even at the risk of her own life, to reverse the horrible edict. She attired herself in her white silken robes, placed a brilliant crown upon her head, gathered her maidens around her, and went boldly and in state to the palace of the King at Shushan.

It was a day of Grand Council, a gathering of the governors, princes and officers of Persia. The dependent nations had sent in their deputations to pay homage and tribute, and the royal guards thronged the ante-chambers of the palace. It was a standing law of that place that none should enter the King's presence without summons, under penalty of death, and the sentinels as the Queen passed reminded her of this and warned her of her danger. But she bade them stand aside, and so, pale but firm, she passed through the vestibule into the great Council Chamber.

The scene was magnificent. The King upon his throne of gold and ivory; the gorgeous equipages of his officers, and the splendor of the apartment itself, all made up a display rarely equaled and never surpassed. Through all the crowd of courtiers ESTHER boldly passed, and amidst the deathly silence of the observers, stood up before the King. Pale with fasting and sleeplessness, but not with fear, her cheeks emulated the whiteness of her silken robes. She fastened her eye fearlessly upon the King, who, angry at the violation of the law, frowned sternly upon her. It was the crisis of her life. The wise woman felt it to be so, and at once reminded him of his former pledges by a method understood between them. She saw his golden scepter bent toward her, and hastened to secure her pardon by coming forward, kneeling and laying her hand upon it. Graciously said the King, " WHAT WILT THOU, Queen ESTHER? and what is thy request? It shall be even given thee to the half

of the kingdom." The admiring crowds applauded
the generosity of their monarch, and as he placed
her beside him on the throne, gave utterance to
loud expressions of admiration at her beauty,
discretion, and favor with the King.

The sacred narrative informs us of the consum-
mate tact with which ESTHER pursued the advantage she had gained. She achieved a complete
success and saved the nation, which, to this day,
keeps an annual festival in her honor.*

---

* A solemn and imposing festival called PURIM, or the *Feast of Lots*,
celebrated by the Jewish people on the 14th and 15th of the month
Adar (corresponding to our month of March), in memory of their
deliverance from the conspiracy of HAMAN by ESTHER.

These lots were cast in the first month of the year, and gave the
twelfth month of the same year for the execution of HAMAN'S design,
to destroy all the Jews in Persia. Thus the superstition of HAMAN, in
crediting these lots, caused his own ruin, and the preservation of the
Jews, who had time to avert this blow, by the influence of ESTHER.
In memory of this deliverance the Jews instituted an annual feast,
which they named Pur, (lots,) or Purim.

This festival is celebrated with every manner of rejoicing and
hilarity, indulging in every kind of rational pleasure and good cheer.
On the eve of the feast they give alms liberally to the poor, that they
may also enjoy the Feast of Lots. On the evening of Adar 13th, when
the feast begins, they assemble in the synagogue, and light the lamps;
and as soon as the stars begin to appear they commence to read the
Book of Esther. There are five places in the text wherein the reader
raises his voice to its highest point. When he comes to the place
which mentions the names of the ten sons of HAMAN he repeats them
very quick, without taking breath, to show that these ten persons were
destroyed in a moment. Every time the name of HAMAN is pronounced
the whole congregation clap their hands, stamp on the floor with their

The color WHITE alludes to the silken robes of ESTHER, emblematical of the spotless purity of her character.

The EMBLEM of the CROWN reminds us of the queenly state of ESTHER, and of the manner in which she hailed the notice of the King.

The SIGN alludes   *   *   *

The PASS is used to recall the grand sacrifice and triumphant success of the heroic ESTHER.

feet, and cry out "Let his memory perish. A custom prevailed in the early practice of these ceremonies to bring into the synagogue a great stone, with the name of HAMAN written on it, and all the while the Book of Esther was being read, they struck it with other stones, till they had beaten it to pieces.

The next day, early in the morning, they repair to the synagogue, where, after they have read that passage of Exodus (xvii., 8–16) wherein is mentioned 'he war of AMALEK, they again read the Book of Esther, with the same ceremonies as before. After quitting the synagogue, they make good cheer at home, and pass the rest of the day and evening in sports and mirth.

They compel every one to be present at the synagogue—men, women, children and servants; because all shared in the benefits of the deliverance which ESTHER obtained for them. On this day scholars make presents to their teachers, heads of families to their domestics, the great to those in mean condition. In a word, the whole day and evening is spent in joyfulness, sports and feasting. As it is said in the Book of Esther, ix., 22: "That they should make them days of feasting and joy, and of sending portions one to another, and gifts to the poor."

TRIBUTE TO ESTHER.

See, oh King, the suppliant one,
Pale and trembling at the throne!
  See the golden crown she bears,
  And the silken robe she wears;
Whiter, brighter than their sheen
Is the woman's soul within!

Mercy's golden wand extend,
While her gentle head shall bend:
  Meekly o'er thy scepter now,
  Pardon, favor, bounty show;
Naught in all thy broad domain
Like the woman's soul within!

THE FOURTH POINT.

---oo✦oo---

MARTHA;

OR, THE SISTER'S DEGREE.

---✦---

𝕿𝔥𝔢 𝕾𝔶𝔪𝔟𝔬𝔩 𝔬𝔣 𝔱𝔥𝔢 𝖀𝔭𝔩𝔦𝔣𝔱𝔢𝔡 𝕳𝔞𝔫𝔡𝔰.

Wildly her hands are joined in form of love,
  As at the Savior's feet the mourner lies;
Beseechingly she raises them above,
  While showers of tear-drops blind her languid eyes;
Then looks and pleads and supplicates his aid
In words that win her brother from the dead.

---✦---

Scriptural Illustration.

And whosoever liveth and believeth in me shall never
die. Believest thou this?—JOHN xi., 26.

---✦---

COLOR—𝕲𝖗𝖊𝖊𝖓.—Represented by the *Pine Leaf*,
emblematical of MARTHA, the faithful sister of Bethany.

EMBLEM :—The Broken Column.

I HAVE SEEN HIS STAR IN THE EAST, AND HAVE COME TO WORSHIP HIM.

F. A. T. A. L.

AND ALTOGETHER blest
    Are those who know the LORD:
The grave will kindly yield its guest
    To his resistless word.

MARTHA.

FOURTH DEGREE.

THE structure of Freemasonry in its obligations, emblems and principles is so peculiar, that we, Master Masons, above all other men, are taught *to respect undeviating faith in the hour of trial.* The great doctrines of Masonry are all borrowed from the Bible. Our devotion to Masonry is chiefly founded upon this, that we believe the Bible to be the Word of GOD, and therefore our principles, which are derived from the Bible, were written by the finger of GOD.

Therefore, when we find in history a person *whose faith in the Redeemer was so fixed and thorough that even the death of her most beloved friend could not shake it,* we seize upon that character as our own. We *adopt* and surround it with fraternal protection. We hail it as a Masonic character, and we claim whatever credit or honor may be associated with it.

Such a character, forcibly delineated, we discover in the Book of John, under the title of MARTHA. And we have so surrounded *the appeal of that noble and heroic woman to her Savior, and her thorough confidence in his omnipotent power,* with emblems, legends and tokens of recognition, as to make of it a section in ADOPTIVE MASONRY.

The history of MARTHA as comprising a Degree of the EASTERN STAR is thus given:

Her brother, LAZARUS, was a resident of Bethany, a man of good standing among his fellow-citizens, and the friend of JESUS CHRIST.

The family, composed of two sisters, MARTHA and MARY, with their brother LAZARUS, seem to have possessed all things needful for a happy life.

Bound up in the love of each other, and blessed with the friendship of him whom to know is "everlasting life," the little group were distinguished from their neighbors by a name that proved how thoroughly their hearts were occupied with divine things. They were "the beloved of the Master, the happy household of Bethany."

Upon an occasion when their Divine guest had gone out, beyond the Jordan, upon a mission of charity, LAZARUS was taken suddenly and violently ill. The terrified sisters hastened to inform JESUS of the fact by a messenger, who was instructed to say, "LORD, behold he whom thou lovest is sick!" They reasonably supposed that so tender a missive could not fail of success. But the SAVIOR returned an ambiguous reply. The "Beloved at Bethany" died and was buried. Four days passed, days shrouded with mourning, still the SAVIOR returned not. The sisters were abandoned to grief, not alone for the loss of their brother, their only earthly protector, but for the unkindness of him upon whom they had leaned as the "Rock of their salvation." Yet MARTHA retained her faith, and trusted in him yet to come and restore the friend they had lost.

At the close of the fourth day, intelligence

reached them that JESUS was returning to Bethany. MARTHA hastened to meet him, fell on her knees before him, raised her hands imploringly toward his face, and, with a voice almost suppressed with emotion, cried aloud: "LORD, if thou hadst been here my brother had not died!" Looking a moment after into his face, and animated by the GOD-like benignity with which he looked down upon her, she added: "But I know that even now whatsoever thou wilt ask of GOD, GOD will give it thee!"

Amazing faith! heroic spirit of confidence in her friend! though her brother had been four days in the embraces of death, and the subject of its corrupting influences—though the weight of watchfulness and sorrow rested heavily upon her spirit as she knelt, her hands wildly raised to heaven—there was a spirit of prophecy in her words which give them a value altogether their own.

Then said JESUS: "Thy brother shall rise again" —testing her faith still further.

She replied: "I know that he shall rise again in the resurrection at the last day."

JESUS said unto her: "I AM THE RESURRECTION AND THE LIFE; he who believeth in me, though he were dead, yet shall he live; and whosoever liveth and believeth in me shall never die. BELIEVEST THOU THIS?"

She answered at once, in the tone and spirit of perfect faith: "Yea, LORD, I believe that thou art the CHRIST, the Son of GOD, which should come into the world!"

The reward of such faith was soon rendered. Taking her by the hand, and passing by their dwelling, where they were joined by MARY, they went to the sepulchre, and, as every reader of Scripture knows, JESUS raised the dead man to life.

The color GREEN alludes to the resurrection of LAZARUS, and, by direct inference, that final and grander resurrection, in the last day. Never does Freemason cast the evergreen sprig into the open grave of his brother but the coming event is thus beautifully foreshadowed.

The BROKEN COLUMN is an EMBLEM of the death of a young man in the vigor of life.

The SIGN alludes   *   *   *

The PASS will recall the spirit of fidelity which characterizes the history of MARTHA.

TRIBUTE TO MARTHA.

Raise thy hands above, sweet mourner,
  Higher, higher, toward the throne!
Ah, he sees thee, hears thy story,
  Hears and feels that plaintive moan.

He has wept for human sorrow—
  Let thy sorrows with him plead;
Raise thy hands in faith, and doubt not
  He hath power o'er the dead.

THE FIFTH POINT.

ELECTA;

OR, THE BENEVOLENT DEGREE.

The Symbol of the Martyr.

Dying, as JESUS died, upon the tree—
  Was ever worthier sacrifice than hers!
Sacred the Cross, the nail, the thorn; for he
  Who suffered has redeemed them from the curse;
Just as she passed to blest eternity
  She plead forgiveness to her murderers.

Scriptural Illustration.

And now I beseech thee, lady, not as though I wrote a new commandment unto thee, but that which we had from the beginning, that we love one another.—2d JOHN, i., 5.

COLOR—**Red.**—Represented by the *Red Rose*, emblematical of the unbounded charity and hospitality practiced by ELECTA.

EMBLEM AND GRIP:—The Cup and Clasped Hands.

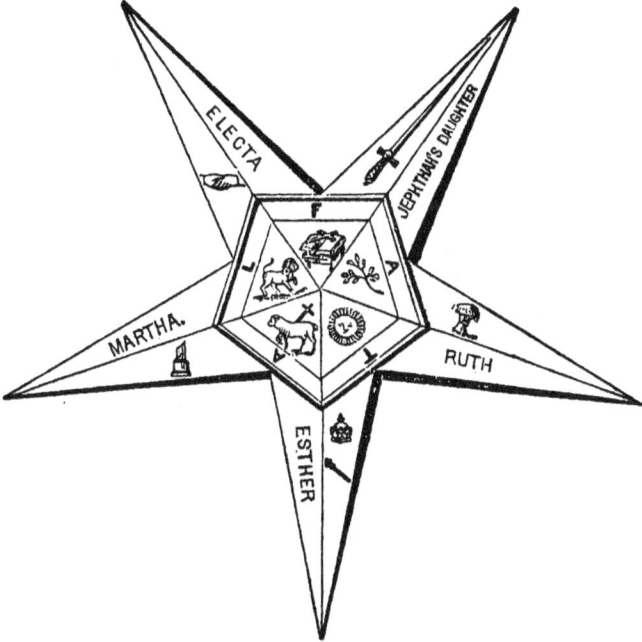

I have seen his Star in the East, and have come to Worship Him.

F. A. T. A. L.

LOVELY upon the shore
    Of Jordan's stream she stands,
Who gave her life for CHRIST and bore
    His witness in her hands.

ELECTA.

FIFTH DEGREE.

THE structure of Freemasonry, in its obligations, emblems and principles, is so peculiar that we, Master Masons, above all other men, are taught to *respect patience and submission under wrongs.* That there will be a day of judgment, when all wrongs shall be redressed by the Divine hand, we firmly believe.

Therefore, when we find in history a person *whose confidence in God's justice gave her perfect patience and submission amidst the most inhuman wrongs*, we seize upon that character as our own. We *adopt* and protect it. We hail it as a Masonic character, and we claim whatever credit or honor may be associated with it.

Such a character, forcibly delineated, we discover in the traditions of our fathers. It is alluded to in the Second Epistle of John, under the title of ELECTA. And we have so surrounded the *submission of that noble and heroic woman under wrong, and her matchless benevolence*, with emblems, legends, and tokens of recognition, as to make of it a section in ADOPTIVE MASONRY.

The history of ELECTA, as composing a Degree of the EASTERN STAR, is thus given:

She was a lady of high repute in the land of Judea, of noble family, wealthy and accomplished, who lived in the days of St. JOHN the Evangelist, and was remarkable for her profuse benevolence to the poor.

ELECTA had been reared, as all her neighbors were, a heathen. The idols of Rome were the only gods she knew. Like RUTH, however, she had been preserved from the abominations of the system, and when by good fortune she was enabled to hear from inspired lips the story of Calvary and its Divine victim, her heart readily opened to the influences of the Holy Spirit. She became converted, together with her husband and all her household. She even professed, *before the world*, her faith in the despised Nazarene, though well she knew that to do so was to expose herself to reproaches, to persecution, and haply to death.

Fourteen years, however, passed away before that great trial came upon her. These years became the happier as well as the better years of her life. She gave her great income to the relief of the poor. Her splendid mansion was made a house of abode to weary and persecuted pilgrims. The poorest of the flock, the tattered, and footsore beggar, coming up the great avenue to her door was met as the father met his prodigal son. She ran out hastily to meet him, took him warmly by the hand, and "welcomed him." She led him to the best apartment, refreshed him with the richest wine in a golden cup, fed, cheered, clothed her guest, nor suffered him to depart until he was strengthened for the journey. Through all the country her name was famous as "the beneficent and affectionate ELECTA." And all this time she was ripening for the better world, and preparing for a fate which, although protracted, was inevitably to settle upon her.

The time of her martyrdom drew nigh. A great persecution began, and any one who had confessed the name of JESUS was required to recant from his faith, or suffer the penalty of the law. ELECTA was visited by a band of soldiers, whose chief officer proposed the test of "casting a cross on the ground and putting her foot upon it," whereupon he would report her recantation. She refused, and the family were cast into a dungeon and kept there one year. Then the Roman Judge came and offered her another opportunity to recant, promising that if she would do so she should be protected. Again she refused, and this brought the drama to a speedy close. The whole family were scourged to the very verge of death. They were then drawn on a cart, by oxen, to the nearest hill, and crucified. She saw her husband perish. She saw each of her sons and daughters die on the cruel tree. She was then nailed there, and being about to pass "to the better land," she prayed with her expiring breath: "Father, forgive them, for they know not what they do!"

The color RED symbolizes *Fervency*, and alludes to the noble generosity of ELECTA, displayed toward the poor and persecuted of her faith.

The EMBLEM of the CUP reminds us of the ardent hospitality of ELECTA, excited by the view of poverty and distress.

The SIGN alludes   *   *   *

The PASS is used to recall the summing up of the grand tragedy which crowned the life of the heroic ELECTA.

The GRIP will serve to remind us of the manner of reception, alike to the rich and poor, practiced by ELECTA.

TRIBUTE TO ELECTA.

When cares press heavy on the heart,
  And all is gloom around,
Where shall we fix the heavy eye
  In all this mortal bound?
What Emblem hath the mourner here?
What love to warm, what light to cheer?

Thine, true ELECTA, thine which tells
  Of his distress and thine!
The CROSS upon whose rugged limbs
  Ye both did bleed and pine!
The CROSS by heavenly wisdom given
To raise our thoughts from earth to heaven.

HE INSTRUCTOR will again refer to the Signet, and repeat, with care and distinctness, the Names, Pass-words, Emblems, Signs, Colors, and Scriptural Passages of each Degree, also the Grip. Induce the ladies to make the Signs, give the Grip, and repeat the Pass-words. Excite a friendly and pleasant spirit of emulation; but keep all in perfect order and good humor. Explain the object and meaning of the motto—"I have seen his Star in the

East, and have come to worship Him"—in the scroll at the top of the Signet. Also, explain in detail the CABALISTIC MOTTO—F. A. T. A. L.— upon the body of the star, in the following or similar language:

JEPHTHAH'S DAUGHTER, because she cheerfully rendered up her life to preserve her father's honor, was . . . . . . RUTH, because she forsook home, friends and wealth, that she might dwell among the people of GOD, was . . . . . . ESTHER, because she was prepared to resign her crown and life to save the people of GOD from death or to perish with them, was . . . . . . MARTHA, because amidst sickness, death and loneliness, she never for a moment doubted the SAVIOR's power to raise the dead, was . . . . . . And finally, ELECTA, because she joyfully rendered up home, husband, children, good name and life, that she might testify to her Christian love by a martyr's death, was . . . . . .

So, ladies, let it be with each of you. As you illustrate the virtues of these chosen and tried servants of GOD, so shall be your reward. You will not be called to suffer as they did, and yet sufferings and trials await all of us in this sublunary state; and those who in the place to which they are called best endure these trials, and resist temptations, prove that had they lived in ancient times they would not have been found wanting, though called to endure as a RUTH or an ELECTA.

As Freemasons, we earnestly solicit your good-will and encouragement in the work in which we are engaged. I have proved to you that it is for your good as much as ours that we are doing the Masonic work. Then, ladies, help us. Help us by defending our principles when you hear them attacked, and by ever speaking a kind word in our behalf. Your smiles and favor are the best encouragement we seek; with them we can do everything, and with them we pledge ourselves to do a double portion for you. And to those kind ladies who thus, while living, prove themselves the friends of Masons and Masonry, we promise that living we will love and respect you, and when you pass from this world to a better we will remember you as . . . .

VALEDICTORY.

Good night! the spirits of the blest and good
   From these dear halls go with you and abide,
In hours of sorrow, hours of solitude,
Or when the hosts of melancholy brood
   And cloud your minds, may angel spirits glide
From the White Throne and give you great delight—
        Dear friends, good night!

Good night, good night! and joy be with you all!
   May sickness never blight, nor poverty:
May slander's breath your spirits ne'er appall;
May no untoward accident befall;
   But all things prosperous and joyful be:
May morning suns rise on you fresh and bright—
        Dear friends, good night!

Good night! in dreams may faithful MARTHA come
   To tell of her beloved, high in heaven;
And RUTH, the gleaner, from her harvest home,
And ADAH, maid immortal from her tomb,
ESTHER and true ELECTA, spirits bright,
        And say, good night!

Good night! and when the shadows of the grave
   Close in around you—when the parting breath
Draws heavily, and unto him who gave
You yield the spirit, be he strong to save
   Who is our guide and SAVIOR unto death:
Then may dear friends and heavenly hopes unite,
        To say, good night!

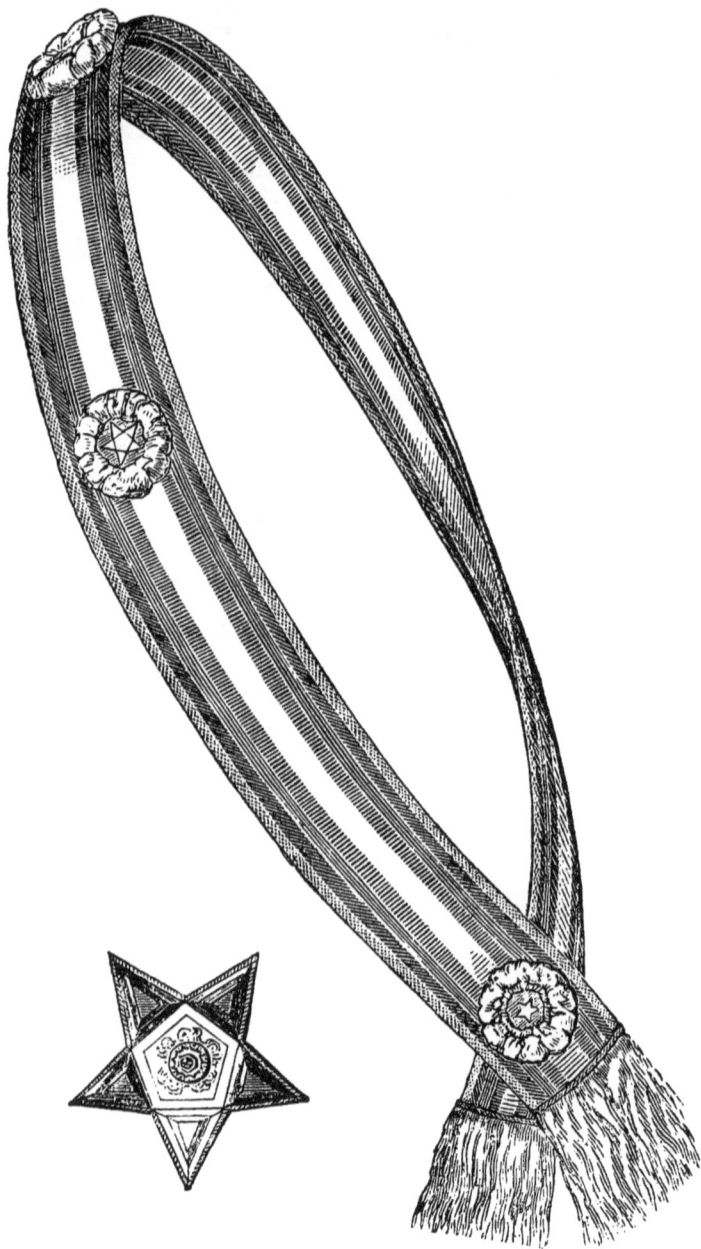

DECORATIONS.

ADIES who receive the Degrees of the EASTERN STAR are entitled to wear, as a decoration, any well-arranged device, emblematical of the Order, and they are earnestly advised to adopt some appropriate BADGE, particularly when traveling, because in case of an accident their claims to the protection of Masons (if any who may have received the Degrees should be present) would be easily recognized.

THE PIN, OR BROOCH,

In the form of a five pointed star, of gold, enameled, or of precious colored stones, may be worn, on all occasions, as a dress ornament.

THE SCARF

Of silk ribbon, three inches wide, the five proper colors woven lengthwise through it, is most appropriate at Masonic festivals, where Masons appear in regalia.

The Scarf should be ornamented with three rosettes; one on the shoulder (flat, of red and blue colored ribbons); one on the breast (quilled, of blue, white, red, yellow and green colored ribbons); one at the crossing (flat, of yellow and green colored ribbons); each rosette ornamented with a five pointed gilt star in the center—the ends of the Scarf to be finished with colored silk fringe.   It is to be worn from right to left.

☞ All communications connected with the Order of the EASTERN STAR, addressed to ROBERT MACOY, National Grand Secretary, 430 Broome street, will receive prompt attention.